Investing in DRIPs

Using Dividend Reinvestment Plans
to Achieve Financial Freedom

THE INCOME INVESTING FOR INDIVIDUALS SERIES

Investing in DRIPs

Using Dividend Reinvestment Plans
to Achieve Financial Freedom

ALAN KERRMAN

First Edition, v. 1.1
Published by Noteable Media
www.dripinvestingplans.com
ISBN-13: 978-1517079260
ISBN-10: 1517079268

Dedication

To my sweetheart and our daughter:
Thanks for giving me the time, space,
and encouragement to write.

Table of Contents

Investing in DRIPs

Using Dividend Reinvestment Plans
to Achieve Financial Freedom

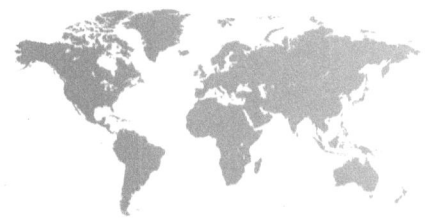

The Power of DRIPs

Compounding Power of Smart Dividend Investing

Here's a book for individual investors, by an individual investor. I've made every mistake there is when it comes to money and investing but I didn't give up. Along the way, I kept hearing about DRIPs (and DSPPs), and I thought that they were some outmoded investment models that went away after the discount brokers gave all of us retail investors a lot more trading choices and features.

NOPE. What I found instead was that DRIPs -- or dividend reinvestment plans -- solved three very serious problems for me! One is that my investing became completely automated. My regular checking account ACH withdrawals meant we'd always make regular monthly investments, and at prices that would dollar-cost-average over the course of the year. Along with the lower fees across the board, this type of income investment also helped me keep from overtrading, saving me all sorts of extra transaction fees. Plus the power of reinvested dividends means compounded growth that we can use for income later when we need it.

Join me as we explore how individual investors now can still take advantage of the power of investing in DRIPs to access the best blue chip companies -- here and around the world -- and get regular dividend payments from a personal portfolio of growth and income stocks. And the best part is that for me, it's part of an overall investment diversification plan that still includes my 401k, my Roth IRA, and a trading account for my stocks, options, and occasional commodity futures. DRIPs now equal compounded dividend income later!

Preface

Dividend Reinvestment Plans (DRIPs) are a system for individual investors to bypass a broker and buy stock directly from a public company in the market. These types of plans are perfect for long-term investors who want to accumulate holdings by making monthly or quarterly purchases of stock. However, with the advent of the discount brokerage account — many with free dividend reinvestment services — many investors consider DRIP plans a thing of the past.

In 2015, DRIP Plans Still Make Sense

Long-term investing in dividend-paying stocks is still considered a smart strategy for individual investors. But retail investors who purchase dividend stocks through their discount brokerage accounts incur transaction fees of an average of $7.99 to $12.99 per purchase. If you buy a dividend-paying stock, this transaction fee essentially wipes out the first few — or several — dividend payments. The other drawback of most brokerage accounts is that you must always make full share stock purchases (1-100+), rather than partial or fractional shares. Outside of a dividend reinvestment plan, you are not allowed to buy half a share of IBM, for example, recently trading at $146.

On the other hand DRIP accounts — after a modest initial set-up fee - often charge as little as $1 or $2 per stock purchase. Some DRIP plans are entirely free, where the underlying company pays all of the necessary fees. In addition to lower transaction costs, DRIP plans, and the related Direct Stock Purchase Plans (DSPPs), allow users to buy fractional shares with each transaction. For example, a monthly purchase of $50 in stock with a debit fee of one dollar would accumulate $49 of the underlying security. A DRIP purchase of stock with a $20 share price would give the investor 2.4500 shares. With regular investing the fractional shares become whole shares, and the desired stock accumulates faster.

The real power of fractional shares happens at the quarterly dividend payout. Dividends are essentially profits being shared by the company with all of its owners, and since you hold shares of the company, you will receive a portion of the profits based on how many shares you hold. The power of DRIP plans is that even the fractional shares earn partial dividends, meaning larger payouts, and at a faster overall rate.

DRIP plans make sense for retail investors for many reasons. It is possible to earn significant dividend income in retirement, but only if you hold a large number of shares. If each share purchase costs about $10 to make, even an occasional $100 investment is weighed down by a ten percent transaction fee. Since the DRIP plans are cheaper all around, it makes sense to make regular monthly purchases and not wait to accumulate a lump sum. Why? When individual investors wait to invest, often the money gets diverted and never ends up in the market.

DRIPs make financial sense. The monthly, quarterly, or annual paperwork requires investors to keep good records but plan on simply buying and

> The power of DRIP plans is that even the fractional shares earn partial dividends, meaning larger payouts, and at a faster overall rate.

reinvesting for a long time. These are not trading accounts. The transfer agents try to dissuade trading of any kind with higher selling fees.

What's the benefit here? These accounts make retail investors plan long-term, and stop trading in and out of their holdings based on news headlines. With steady stock purchases in a DRIP plan over a long period, investors will enjoy the benefit of dollar-cost-averaging: buying less stock when prices are high, and accumulating more when the markets pull back. With the right underlying stocks, DRIP plans are a great long-term wealth plan, even in the volatility of our recent markets.

Introduction

Thanks for reading my new book. As an individual investor who has started to pay more attention to his finances over the last few years, I felt compelled and empowered to learn about all the available resources at my fingertips. This journey eventually led me back to DRIPs (dividend reinvestment plans). Many people — if they've even heard of DRIPs at all — think they're an outmoded strategy with no benefit for the modern investor.

Not true. DRIPs are incredibly timely and give an insight into what individual investors should be focused. I think about the ways a DRIP or DSPP (direct stock purchase plans) fits into a present-day portfolio and sharing that with you is the principal goal of writing this book. So, my fellow individual investor, this book is for you!

This book contains up-to-date information and discussions about:

- You'll find the reasons why you should at least consider DRIPs or DSPP plans for a portion of your overall long-term investing strategy. It has a place in your family's 21st-century wealth building and retirement plans.

- What exactly DRIPs are, the powerful secrets embedded into their design, and why most online brokers don't want you to understand them.

- How to go about investing in DRIPs and DSPPs — both in terms of the basics, and also some individual portfolio strategy and diversification considerations.

- And the WHAT IF! We also take a look at some actually money $$$ examples of DRIP investing spun out over time by investors of various ages to get an idea what kind of returns might be possible.

> I love DRIPs, and I still get excited each time I see my dividend payments coming in.

I'm an individual retail investor just like you, and I wrote this short book to share a little bit about DRIPs (dividend reinvestment plans) and DSPPs (direct stock purchase plans). I am not a finance professional or registered investment advisor. I don't even work in the financial field at all. I am just a guy who wants to know that his long-term retirement plan is on track and that I will be able to be able to provide for my wife and daughter long into the future. With that, I am fascinated by investing, personal finance, the stock market, and wealth building, and I care enough to roll up my sleeves and learn all I can. (So do you, or you wouldn't be reading this!)

I love DRIPs, and I still get excited each time I see my dividend payments coming in. (I know, it's a little silly, but it's fun to see this entire plan in motion.) I think there's room for DRIPs in everyone's portfolio, and among everyone's assets. But that's up to you to decide after you see what's here. (As I mention in the disclaimer on the copyright page, please consult your advisors and other professionals before committing any risk capital to any investment, including dividend reinvestment plans.) I also recommend that you fully understand every asset the you invest in. It is easier than it seems.

At my full-time day job teaching at a university, I have access to a 403b retirement account. This means that the bulk of my assets is in traditional mutual funds with a couple different investment firms. As long as I stay with my current job, I'll continue to make these regular paycheck contributions, augmented by a small employer match. Like a 401K, the 403b is a retirement asset that grows tax-deferred, meaning that I will only pay taxes later, as I take distributions from the account at retirement age. For me, that point is at least a couple decades away, or maybe longer.

I tell you about my 403b plan because this process is generally how most people save for retirement. We select a pre-tax deduction amount (or a percentage) from our paycheck and have that money taken out automatically each pay period. Usually, we'll visit the retirement plan website at least once, and select some mutual funds (filled with stocks or bonds). Many investors rarely at their assets look again until the annual statement.

(In case you're wondering, for my contributions I choose to invest a percentage of my bi-weekly paycheck so that when I get periodic pay raises, my contributions to my retirement account increase automatically.)

Okay, solid. Again, this is what most people do… but I'm covering this to make a specific point. Let's talk about fees.

Fees

One of the funds that I have in my seemingly well-diversified account is Fidelity's Contrafund (symbol: FCNTX). As you know mutual funds are simply baskets of stocks, then split into shares so that many investors can participate in a wide array of investments. As of this writing, a single share of the Contrafund costs just over $100, and it counts Berkshire Hathaway Inc (BRK-A), Wells Fargo & Co (WFC), Apple (AAPL), Facebook (FB), Google Inc (GOOGL, GOOG), Biogen Idec, Inc (BIIB), and Disney Co (DIS), among its top holdings. It's considered a large cap growth fund, meaning most of its holdings are very big growth-oriented companies.

At this point, I'm happy having some of my retirement assets in the widely-respected Fidelity Contrafund.

But here's the problem. According to the Morningstar website, this fund has a net expense ratio of 0.66%, which is low and reasonable as far as actively-managed mutual funds go. Those fees pay the salaries, overhead costs, and administrative expenses related to managing that fund. I get it.

But according to Morningstar's projections, an investor with $10K invested would likely pay around $798 in fees over a 10-year period holding this fund. (Or about $205 over three years, or about $357 over five years.)

Okay. So what's the big deal? Well, we all know that we need WAY more than $10K to retire! And it's possible that you easily could contribute $5K per year just into this one fund.

What's your long-term investment goal? To meet your retirement needs, what balance do you need in your retirement accounts? Even if you don't know an exact number, assume that it's at least $500,000 to $1,000,000. To get to that level by retirement, you might be well on your way to six figures in assets at this point. So for example — if you're holding $100K now (in this single fund for example), you'd pay over $8350 over the next decade, or well over $16K over the next 20 years!! [I know, we're skipping the compounding for the second decade, but this is mind-boggling!] And this is for a fund considered to have relatively low fees…

What's your long-term investment goal?

[Yes, I'm well-diversified in my investments, and could never imagining keeping $100K in a single fund. But okay, if you must know, I currently have about $15K in this individual fund, meaning I'm likely paying $1197 in fees over the next decade — all $$$ that comes right out of the growth of my investment. That averages out to $120 a year, or $9.98 per month just for this. Uggh! Do the math! If you have six more funds like this you could be paying $60 per month or more in retirement account fees!] (And remember that most actively-managed funds do not actually beat the performance of the market!)

By the way, this fee discussion makes the argument for index funds, which I think are a very good idea, but that's for another book! The well-respected Vanguard 500 Index Fund [VFINX] currently has an expense ratio of 0.17%, which works out to about $217 per $10K over ten years, or $2170 on $100,000. Much cheaper, of course, but that's just to track the market automatically!

These fee discoveries made me consider new ways to invest long-term, which led me to... active TRADING. (Thought I would say DRIPs? Nope, not yet.)

I'll keep this brief, but trading is still something I do. Stocks, options, futures, forex — I've tried it all but settled on stocks and options with a dabbling in index and commodities futures. But while I was learning about ACTIVE TRADING, I also started thinking more about transaction fees, and the very common problem of overtrading.

As I kept reading about finance, trading and investing, I stumbled on DRIPs. Initially, I saw dividend reinvestment as a simple service that the discount brokers like E*Trade, Scottrade, and TD Ameritrade seemed to offer for free. What was the big deal?

Well, you'll find out here that what was once a very popular way to invest is still relevant, and possibly regaining its appeal. And you'll also find out that DRIP plans operating directly through a company — and its transfer agent — are completely different than the courtesy reinvestments regularly done by discount brokers. And the full DRIPs have other serious benefits.

So let's get started...

1

......

My Very Personal Finance

I t's not hard to believe that the whole modern finance industry is set up to rob us all blind. We're expected to be complete idiots, and just stroll into the propellor of ignorance. Read between the lines of many stock recommendations by CNBC/Bloomberg talking heads, celebrity finance writers, and rock-star hedge fund dudes, and you'll see this constant pattern of "buy this, I already did!"

Sure that's easy.

If I own something cheap(er) and then encourage everyone to pile in, that just drives the price up, and I could sell soon after. That "pump and dump" is pretty common for speculative stocks, but even if the recommending party doesn't "dump" their shares, the added interest provides a nice little buffer of safety. For them...

So, yeah this isn't your typical finance book. And it's not a book by a Wall Street insider. And no, I'm not a registered investment advisor. This book is my opinion, my reflections, and my insights based on years of my own personal investing, trading, and overall financial experiences.

And it's a very personal journey for me. Personal finance is very, very personal to me (keep reading and you'll see why!)

And other than this cheap little book (thanks again for reading this!), I'm not selling you anything. I don't have some paid course, or an investment fund, or some fee-based training program. Nope. (I do have a little DRIP-related blog where this all started, but that's not really to make money!)

I'm not a finance professional at all — I work in higher ed. But I've dedicated so much time, energy, effort, and struggle to build a great future for my family, that I want to share with you exactly what I've figured out -- individual investor to individual investor...

But the truth is that I'm much more motivated than most individual investors. (Yes, even more than you!)

I'm more motivated about money and finance because I'm not just saving up for a comfortable retirement and just looking out for my family. I'm not just trying to master our assets to make sure we never run out of money long-term, or to be able to give money to charity and help others. Nope, I serious about this stuff because I made a promise (about money) that I need to keep.

And I will keep that promise...

My Very Personal Family Story of Love, Loss, and Money

Let me share a personal story... and yes, it's true — and in case you're wondering — yes it's very hard to write this.

Why? Because at a time when I didn't need the money for anything specific, I had received a lump sum insurance inheritance from my father who passed away. It was about ten years ago, and my life was completely different. I made some pretty naive, and pretty stupid choices with that money — and I have now serious regrets and serious goals.

Here's our story: My family had some real financial ups and downs when we were growing up, but I remember my father working unbelievably hard at two jobs to break that cycle. My parents later split up, my mom disappeared with her new boyfriend, and my dad did everything he could to make our lives better. He worked so hard - day and night! Dad later remarried, and my sister and I could tell that a new chapter had begun. With his continued drive and hustle, my father finally achieved a serious degree of financial stability — with money in the bank and some real estate — and he wanted to share with us what he had learned.

The truth is that I'm much more motivated than most individual investors.

I have so much respect for my father for turning our lives around, and I'm still amazed that he pulled it off. He inspires me to this day. He is also the smartest man I've ever known. I wanted to know what he knew — not just to be comfortable or to make money — but to honor his struggles, and let him share with me what he learned. Passing on knowledge like that would change our 'family tree,' as financial guru Dave Ramsey always says.

I wanted to learn...

[Even as an adult, my older sister didn't care to learn about investing, finance, or real estate. (Sadly, against all helpful advice, counsel, and pleading, she still does wacky things with her money! For example, she changed jobs a few years back, and instead of rolling over her 401k, she just cashed it out, paid huge early-withdrawal penalties and income taxes, and used it to pay off some stupid credit card debt! She effectively reset her retirement assets to ZERO ($0!) in her thirties! Ahhhhh!??! And that silly credit card debt was built up by spending on stuff like clothes, gas, dog food, and restaurant outings, and then by missing payments!)]

I told my father that I wanted to learn about money and investing, which was true, but I was also bull-headed, just out of college. I was living with my crazy girlfriend, and trying to find my place in the world. And I was pretty distracted by my life, my career choices, and my growing relationship drama.

But I loved stocks! (He and I bought Lucent Technologies together as my first stock purchase because my father believed that their patents were more valuable than the company's stock price (or overall market capitalization). We were wrong on (now) the Alcatel-Lucent [ticker: ALU] investment. But his strategy of looking for 'hidden' intellectual property (IP) value was later proven correct on many other large buyouts in technology!)

My father would try to pass along his accumulated financial knowledge during family visits — over multiple cups of tea (with milk) — over the telephone, at family holidays — or literally whenever we found time to get together. But adult life is funny that way... My long-term relationship turned into a short marriage, and she and I went our separate ways. My life was weird, and then my Dad life's got very complicated. He got divorced (again), lost assets, got depressed, lost more assets, got sick, lost more assets, and later died... way, way too soon.

In the end, he died with very few assets (between the second divorce and his illness), but he left something specific for me. One last asset, and his hopes for it...

Instead of listing his last substantial asset (a long-standing insurance policy) as going to both children, he wanted it to go 100% to me. Why? He wanted me to take it, honor his remaining small debts and IOUs, and then build that money into a large lump that would later benefit both of us. He wanted me to manage it, grow it, invest it, and then (much) later send my sister small, regular payments — hopefully for the rest of our lives.

I promised my father when he was sick that I would do these things. I would take care of all of it. This all would be rebuilt and would help my life, and I would also provide ongoing help to my older sister with this asset.

But he was very sick, and I just wanted to spend time with him, so we didn't talk about finances very much. If we did, that would signal that the end was close, and I couldn't admit that. He was also very private and didn't want anyone to know what he had decided. But he died too soon, and after my unbelievable grief, I was very cloudy about how to proceed. In retrospect, I wish he had been much more specific about how to handle this money — I really should have asked! (Instead he gave me books… I later devoured them, and many, many others!)

But I messed up… Nope, no gambling, no race track, no fancy car, but perhaps worse…

(Any of you have regrets when it comes to money?)

Biggest Money Mistakes

So let me first say that I later tracked (or at least looked back) some of the missed opportunities, and realized that almost every other idea that I had — and gave up on — would have been better than what I eventually did.

I moved nearly all the remaining assets — large amounts of cash in my world — into a 4X margin trading account at E*Trade. What that means is that they let me trade — intraday — on four times my available cash. This "plan" was ridiculous! I specifically remember day-trading more than a quarter million dollar Google stock position, and risking multiples of my annual salary intraday!

…risking multiples of my annual salary intraday!

Well, let me first say that if you get any large lump sum of money, please wait longer than 90 days to make any big decisions! The funeral was in the winter, and the grief hit me hard, but by spring I had a 6-figure check in my hands. It actually came registered mail, so when I went to the local post office to sign for it, I remember sitting in my crappy car in their parking lot and crying as I opened the envelope. I didn't want the money — I just wanted one more day with him. I didn't want my life to change in this way.

I have lost so much money in the market it's a wonder that I still go anywhere near stocks! There I said it. I still have capital losses that I roll over each year on my taxes. (In case you're wondering, it's only a $3k a year deduction max, and the rest carries forward. And yes, I even tried writing to congressmen to introduce a bill to increase that amount! Talk about the horses already out of the gate...)

But assets move, and tides ebb and flow, so even with all of my pain and misery in the markets, I probably have 75% of it back! (Remember, I'm an educator... What? 75% that's a 'C' average! Why listen to someone with a C average?)

You decide. My pain is now on display in the hard-won battle scars of experience. (Like all of us!) This book is my mini-tell-all. From individual investor to individual investor — here's my book about DRIPs, and DSPPs, and how they fit into a bigger financial picture of stocks, mutual funds, trading, real estate, and more — and the best practices.

P.S.: In case you're wondering... YES, I'm glad that I didn't lose the money gambling at the racetrack, the casino, or playing poker or something extra painful and stupid. Because I lost money legitimately in the stock market, I have a mechanism for tax deductions, and the 'benefit' of earning it back tax-free. That's my only salvation. Plus the "education" I received from those mistakes was priceless, or very, very expensive depending on how you look at it.

But all of that said, DRIPs are the plan to get it all back on track, and to do what my father wanted. I could even set up a couple large DRIPs for my sister, and send her all the dividends...

So let's dive in...

2
......

About Investing in DRIPs

Usually when people hear about investing in DRIPs (dividend reinvestment plans), they try to compare it to the excitement and possible returns that come from chasing growth stocks. The truth is that these two investing strategies are opposite. If you are attempting to become financially free and live mainly on dividend income, you must understand the difference.

Simply stated, growth stocks are the hot companies with products or services that are currently doing very well, moving fast and become widely known by providing new popular products or services to consumers. (Of course, growth companies can stay in that mode for many years.) Wall Street rewards these companies by speculating on their FUTURE product cycles, innovation, and growth prospects. It also rewards them for their talent and innovative leadership, forward-thinking management, and angel investors. But in some cases and with some red-hot companies in the news, those long-term growth prospects never arrive. That's fine.

But for momentum traders, and longer-term swing traders, the price of a growth stock like that can double, triple, or grow many times over during one of these accumulation periods when everybody has to own the stock. Many, many people profit during this buy low and sell high phase of a stock's ascent. And even the founders, employees, and early investors in companies like these benefit — they rode the way for a while, made some money, and can simply move on to the next start-up idea. Which solar, biotech, chip manufacturer, internet company will make it in those competitive landscapes? Who is the Apple, Facebook, Google, Genentech, Tesla, or First Solar of 2025?

But for growth and momentum traders and investors, the problem (or art, if you will) is always about when exactly to sell their holdings? (Making a trade INTO an investment is usually a good way to go broke, but that's another story...)

> ...without actively getting in at the right time, and exiting with a profitable sale, it can be tough for retail investors to make money on these types of momentum growth stocks.

A recent and relevant example of this is the company Tesla Motors (ticker symbol: TSLA). The story of this electric car company, with its youthful visionary CEO, has been a Wall Street darling for a while. If you bought a single share of the stock today, it would cost you about $195 per share. On January 3, 2014, it was just under $150. Nice return if you bought it at the beginning of the year and sell it now!

Why? Because the only way to profit from the stock (except selling options) is to sell it and take the capital gain. But if you bought TSLA in late September of 2013, you could have paid $190 per share, and you be up a few dollars. Of course, perhaps you bought the stock in April of 2013 at only $51, a great buy! Would you sell at $100 two months later? My point here is that without actively getting in at the right time, and exiting with a profitable sale, it can be tough for retail investors to make money on these types of momentum growth stocks.

I'm not saying it can't be done; it's just hard. If you bought TSLA at $50 and sold at $100, would you feel comfortable buying again at $150, even though we now see the upside in that decision. And who is buying now or six months from now?

Is it too late?

The 52-week range for Tesla has been from a low of about $177 to as high as $291. In retrospect, it's easy to see the exits, but also possible to own a growth stock like this from a much higher entry point and be completely underwater with no recourse.

Dividend Payers

But unlike pure growth stocks, I prefer to find solid companies with earnings, income, and modest growth that ALSO pay dividends and regularly share their business profits with the owners. And as a shareholder, we are obviously partial owners — no matter how small — and we are entitled to dividend payments or a share of the business profits. Will you make that astounding 100% return in two months with a growth and income stock? Nope, probably not. Can you still lose money? Of course. But stocks that pay dividends tend to have more "loyal" investors who know they will get paid quarterly so many will not sell even if the company has a bad earnings report or has announced some unfavorable news. The company is rewarding us for owning the stock by sharing the earnings. And the smart companies know that this breeds loyalty.

The first step obviously is to learn about these DRIP and DSPP plans as a way to own and hold dividend paying stocks, and consider how they fit into your overall long-term financial plan.

This book will explain the journey that led me to invest in DRIPs (effectively!), and will serve as a guide to prepare you for a foundation of long-term financial success. There is a handful of things one should prepare before attempting to invest in dividend stocks. So before investing in drips, you first should assess your overall financial situation and make certain that you're prepared to invest at all.

These are questions you need to ask yourself:

- Do you know exact how much you earn and where all of that money goes each month?
- Do you have feeling that aspects of investing are too difficult to learn?
- Would you like to automate aspects of your financial matters?
- Do you want to avoid chasing today's volatile stocks?

If you answered "yes" to these questions then most likely investing in DRIP plans is an appropriate strategy.

Before we get started with what you **NEED TO KNOW** about investing in dividend reinvestment plans, we will cover the basics as you prepare to start this fun and exciting journey. (I don't know about you, but I think it's fun to watch my money, assets, and portfolio grow each month or each year!) After all, financial planning is an important step for you and your family - and it's a journey of the spirit, body, and mind. It gets you thinking about many, many years in the future, and then going back to enjoying your life in the here and now. It is logical that you must prepare for this journey before taking the plunge into DRIP or DSPP investing.

Here are some tips to start you off:

1 - Choose established companies

Choosing stocks of established companies is one thing that someone looking to invest in DRIP plans should always do. If you are already used to investing in some dividend-paying stocks, then you understand the benefit of companies that pay you quarterly. DRIPs and DSPPs are not for speculative investments, although less of those companies even offer direct investing.

2 - Saving for retirement

Part of the discipline that is required to prepare for investing in DRIPs involves already saving for retirement. When you save for retirement — planning for the support of your future you — you're in the appropriate mindset for long-term investing. You also have other retirement assets to offset the nondiversified nature of DRIP investing. For example — like my story— if you have a 401K or 403b at work, and you invest in a mix of growth and income mutual funds as well as bond funds, then it's obviously not too dangerous to have a single DRIP investment in IBM (International Business Machines) stock, for example.

3 - Planning for financial independence

One of the biggest mistakes that people make when it comes to preparing to invest is ignoring this step. If you do not plan for your overall financial independence, it will be next to impossible to meet that goal. Where does your money come from? What assets will you accumulate? How long do you need to continue to work? What personal and family expenditures will you have besides your retirement (for example a wedding, travel, higher education, long-term care, etc.)?

So, let's get started...

I don't know about you, but I think it's fun to watch my money, assets, and portfolio grow each month or each year!

3
......

Investing in DRIPs:
Step by Step

Undoubtedly, the first thing you should do before you invest — especially after-tax investing — is to make sure that you have created your monthly budget. I believe this is essential in verifying that you are ready to invest in **DRIP** plans. Many people think that even without a budget they have a pretty good idea of all the money matters in their household. It's not true.

It's almost impossible - unless you track every source of income and expense for at least a month or two — to know what your money is doing. And creating your monthly budget (tracker) has several benefits. For one, it immediately shows you how much you can invest. You need always to know the big picture with your money matters. On a positive note, most people discover that with a closely tracked budget they can invest **MORE** than they were planning to.

How?

Well if you find any waste, unnecessary expenses, or redundancies, then you can earmark that money for your dividend stock portfolio. If you had to guess the amount of money you could devote to an investment plan, would it be too conservative? Or would you find that your budget is too tight to handle additional monthly outflow, and you have decisions to make. This is all critical information to know.

Over time, the more money you use to buy assets that will create income — through dividends — the more your money is now working for you. Also, creating any monthly budget results in taking control of your finances which is a key to getting ahead over the long term.

Credit card debt and other revolving debt accounts

It's hard to talk about long-term goals without tackling the problem of debt. I have a friend who never seems to make any traction in this area. He and his wife have been completely strangled by credit card, revolving, and medical debt for at least fifteen years.

Do you need to be completely out of debt to begin investing?

Paying off any credit card or revolving debt is essential to successfully invest in dividend stocks as well. There are numerous benefits to this; however some retail investors are motivated alone by realizing that the monthly credit card interest alone could build a serious DRIP account! And lowering your overall debt-to-income ratio is important to gaining that overall level of financial stability and peace of mind that I consider critical. Without gaining this stability — and most people don't — you will always feel like a slave to your bills and your debts.

Do you need to be completely out of debt to begin investing? Not necessarily, although some personal finance gurus believe that you should delay investing until all your debts are eliminated. I think you do both, and the motivation to grow your investment accounts will make you aggressively pay down your debts.

Debt is fascinating too... It's also a very clear argument that anyone can invest. Why?

According to some sources including the Federal Reserve, an average amount between $7,000 to $15,000 is carried in credit card debt by every US household. Add to that a staggering $33K in average student loan debts, and about $156K (or more!) in mortgage debt, and you see why many believe that they can't invest now for the long-term.

With an average credit card interest rate (at the time of this writing) between 13-16%, that $7K debt looks like this:

- At 13% interest, to pay off a $7K balance in 3 years (36 months), the monthly payment would need to be: $235.86
- At 16% interest, to pay off a $7K balance in 3 years (36 months), the monthly payment would need to be: $246.10
- At 13% interest, to pay off a $7K balance in 2 years (24 months), the monthly payment would need to be: $332.79
- At 16% interest, to pay off a $7K balance in 2 years (24 months), the monthly payment would need to be: $342.74
- At 13% interest, to pay off a $7K balance in 1 years (12 months), the monthly payment would need to be: $625.22
- At 16% interest, to pay off a $7K balance in 1 years (12 months), the monthly payment would need to be: $635.12

(Keep those numbers in mind if you're thinking about getting a car payment! You could delay any financed vehicle purchase and pay off this sort of household credit card debt in the same amount of time! Drive a used car like many wealthy people do!)

When we started investing in DRIPs, we started developing a pretty serious monthly budget and tracking system, and we started to find extra money for both our debts and extra investing! It can be done... We found MORE money to pay down our debt, AND we found more money to contribute to our monthly DRIP plans. It also inspired me to moonlight a little (side jobs!) to make extra money to kill our debt or raise our investing. (I'd rather work extra now rather than when I'm 80!)

So hidden inside your monthly budget is that additional money to pay down those debts faster and to build a DRIP portfolio that will pay you back for years to come. In a later chapter, we will look (conservatively) at how even a small monthly contribution can result in a sizable account balance later.

Of course, wiping out credit card debt has a way of lowering all our stress at home, and that's an amazing side-effect. You'll feel more relaxed about money, and it gives you the headspace to plan for building assets long-term. Decide now to track all the money that comes in and out of your household for an entire month, and you'll be very surprised about what you find.

All the while you can start thinking about which DRIP plan to start with. Do you want to own a retail company like Wal-Mart Stores (ticker symbol: WMT), which currently pays a 2.40% dividend, or maybe a technology company like Intel Corporation (ticker symbol: INTC) which pays a 3.10% dividend. Or maybe you have enough funds free to choose a small portfolio of DRIPs, so you could get both of these two stocks and a food company like Kellogg Company (ticker symbol: K), which also pays a 3.1% dividend. (Of course, you likely know that the dividend yield is calculated by the annual payout divided by the current stock price, which is why the percentage yield posted online frequently changes. For example, a company that pays a quarterly dividend of $0.25 per share ($1.00 annually) and with a $100 stock price, gives us a 1.00% dividend yield ($1.00/$100.00=1.00%). With the same stock trading lower at $94, but still paying $0.25 quarterly ($1.00 per year), the dividend yield becomes 1.06%.)

Now let's get to the secret benefits of DRIP investing...

4

......

'How To' and the Secret Benefits of DRIPs

I call this chapter the secret benefits because this is all of the information about DRIPs that I had to learn and see for myself that wasn't readily explained, or even available out there when I was getting started. If it was available information, it wasn't often presented in ways that we later found pretty useful.

How to Actually Invest in DRIPs

But before we get to that let's talk about HOW TO INVEST IN DRIPs. It's pretty easy, and each one of the transfer agent companies makes it easy. But let's make it into an easy list:

1. Decide on a company that you're interested in. Try their company website (Google it!), and look at their Investor Relations page and look for their FAQ (frequently asked questions). You're looking for mention of a DRIP plan, direct investing, or a DSPP (direct stock purchase plan.) If you can't find a candidate this way, visit the sites listed on our resources page — ComputerShare, Wells Fargo ShareOwner Services, and others, and choose a stock from their list where they already manage the company's plan.

2. How do you decide? Check the minimum investment, consider the sector and industry, and read about the fees. (Sadly many more of these DRIPs apparently used to be completely free, but some are not, so consider that when you invest. They are ALL cheaper than most discount brokers, so even with fees the benefits are powerful.)

3. Open a new account at the transfer agent (resources page), and give them the owner's name, address, and investment amount. Some plans have a one-time admin set-up fee — make note of those. With some of these plans, you can avoid a minimum (say $500 or $1000 now), by committing to several automatic bank transfer electronic payment investments (ACH - "automated clearing house"). This is how I started with my first DRIP. We chose Kellogg & Co (ticker: K), no fees and agreed to a debit of $50 per month. Kellogg is in the Consumer Goods sector, and in the Processed & Packaged Goods Industry. (You can find that information about any company at Yahoo Finance.) It's that simple.

> This is how I started with my first DRIP.

4. Then choose how you want your quarterly dividends handled. We chose 100% reinvestment. That way every penny of dividend income we earned is immediately turned into more fractional shares. But of course, you could receive these payments as cash (bank transfer, checks, etc.) in either full or partial amounts. This way as you get closer to retirement age, you might decide to reinvest 50% of your dividends and get the rest deposited into your checking account. For example, Kellogg pays a quarterly dividend of $0.49 per share. If you hold 500 shares (worth about $31K in today's market), the quarterly dividend would be $245, or $980 per year. If you reinvest, you're getting about four more shares with each payout, or about 16 new shares a year at current prices.

5. Finally, you can choose how you want to handle your paperwork. We do everything online, so I chose electronic statement, asking only for paper statements annually and our tax forms. (Yes, dividends are taxable even if you reinvest them, but it's less than taxes on earned income, so I'd rather reinvest and cover any taxes due.)

6. That's it, and you have a DRIP plan or DSPP plan. So if you had diversified assets elsewhere, a single plan could be enough. After maxing out all of your tax-deferred, and tax-free investing strategies, you could put any additional money here.

So here's what makes DRIPs so powerful and interesting... my so called 'secrets' list!

SECRET NUMBER ONE:

When you own stocks directly from the company (or its transfer agent), the ownership is actually in your name. (When you own them at your broker, they are often listed in your account, but still owned by your platform.) There are some benefits here from more direct access to company events (shareholder meetings, perks, etc.), but also a level of 'intention' that comes from really owning something. Many investors will spend hours and days researching a vacation (an experience!), or a new car (a depreciating asset), but will choose a stock investment (initially hundreds or even thousands of dollars) on a whim, a tip, or a hunch.

SECRET NUMBER TWO:

The entire collective finance industry seems to want to keep DRIPs a secret for some reasons. Mostly because of the simplicity and the lower fee structure — I presume. But even when DRIPs or DSPPs are discussed, it is often as an 'outmoded' model of investing, or a function already covered by the DRIP functions (reinvestments) at the retail brokerages.

SECRET NUMBER THREE:

Related to the previous statement, DRIPs widely reduce the need and possibility for overtrading, which is one of the drags on long-term return rates. Why? Regardless of your investment timeline, it will put you onto a slower moving plan. These holdings are part of your buy-and-hold strategy and will keep your income-generating assets on track. (If that's not a concern, and you still want to trade actively — the DRIP portfolio is a diversified hedge against other styles, strategies of investing.)

SECRET NUMBER FOUR:

More of your money goes towards your ownership. Think about it — even if your discount broker transaction fees are only $7.99 for each buy and sell, if you 'churn' your account too often, a lot of your gains (if any) are lost to slippage. In the case of the General Electric (ticker: GE) DRIP, for example, each purchase costs $1 from the transfer agent.

SECRET NUMBER FIVE:

The compounding is the whole amazing aspect of leverage here, obviously. All of my current shares and all of my reinvested dividends help create new shares and dividends. This is a much faster way to build up assets. And with the lower fees of the previous paragraph, every dollar (minus transaction costs) goes towards your investment. If my stock costs $112 per share, and I'm only investing $100 per month in this DRIP, I will still get almost a full share each month. Try that with your discount broker -- try to buy 89% of a share of stock! You can't.

> The ratio of the transaction cost to your overall investment is low.

SECRET NUMBER SIX:

The ratio of the transaction cost to your overall investment is low. For example, if I want to buy $300 worth of GE, and I spend $1 in fees with the transfer agent, I'll get $299 worth of shares — out to three or four decimal places. That makes my cost 0.33% of my transaction. If I pay $7.99 for the same shares at my online broker, I'd be able to only buy 11 shares (at the recent price of $25.45), and would only spend $279.95 on stock. But that nearly $8 fee is a full 2.85% of my money — lost to slippage and transaction costs. Additionally, the stock cost for 11 shares $279.95 plus the 7.99 transaction fee (equaling $287.94) leaves $12.06 that I was ready to spend but couldn't. It would also take — with only 11 shares — three quarterly dividend payments of 11 shares times

$0.23 — or $2.53 to earn back the $7.99 we spent to buy our shares. At $1 fee, the first dividend payment (higher than $2.53 because of the extra fractional shares) would fully cover our entry costs. This is also what makes investors in discount brokers wait for larger sums before they invest. Instead of buying 11 shares of GE this month, why not buy 22 next month? What you'd find is that $600 could afford 23 shares (assuming that it's still at our current price.) So 23 shares x $25.45 (current price) is $585.35. Add our $7.99, and we're using $593.34 and still leaving $6.36 uninvested. But even at $7.99 for our invested $585 (for 23 shares), it's still 1.36% in fees. (Embedded fees are that scary hidden variable in mutual funds and bonds, but that's a different book!)

SECRET NUMBER SEVEN:

Automatic investing is powerful — and calming. What I like most about setting up a monthly plan is that I will dollar-cost-average my basis price throughout the year. For example, Walmart (ticker: WMT) is currently trading at about $83 (Mar 2015), but in November, December, January it was trading around $86, $88, and a high of almost $91 in January. (Use Yahoo! Finance historical prices to see a big overview of stock prices. Of course, if you bought all of your shares in December, you would have paid around $85 for Walmart. But if you bought some every month of the last year, you'd have shares at $74, $77, $75, $73, $72, $74, $75, $75, $86, $85, $84, and $83, plus reinvested dividends. (Even that list has an average price of $77.75, better than the current price.) It keeps you from market timing, and amazingly you start to feel confident whether the market goes up ("my portfolio is growing!!") or down ("I'll get some cheap shares this month!").

> # You start to feel confident whether the market goes up or down.

SECRET NUMBER EIGHT:

This is one of my favorite revelations about DRIPs! You buy shares, earn your dividends, and essentially — over time — will get all your money back. Huh? Think about it: One share of GE is $25.45, plus $1 (minus one-time set-up costs) is a cost of $26.45. At $0.23 per share quarterly dividend — and without dividend increases — you will get all your money back in 115 quarters, or 28.75 years. And that's with cash. If you let your dividends get reinvested, it's much faster.

SECRET NUMBER NINE:

With a little digging online, it's easy to find out the dividend payment cycles for these DRIP stocks. So what we've tried to do it choose stocks — as part of our sector, industry, and other diversification — that pay different months during the year. You can have a holding that pays in JAN-APR-JUL-OCT, and another that pays in FEB-MAY-AUG-NOV, and a third that pays in MAR-JUN-SEP-DEC, and receive dividends every month of the year.

JAN	APR	JUL	OCT
FEB	MAY	AUG	NOV
MAR	JUN	SEP	DEC

At first, when these dividends are on reinvestment, you won't notice that cycle as much, but at some point when you turn off that part and take the dividend deposits or checks as income, you may appreciate the schedule.

Now let's take a look at a small sampling from the wide range of companies that offer these plans...

5

......

DRIP Stocks Today: What Stocks Can I Buy?

Here is a very small sampling of companies that have direct stock purchase plans (DSPP) and/or dividend reinvestment plans (DRIP) available right now. This partial list is to inspire you to choose stocks to hold in your accounts for the long-term, but always, be sure to check the fees, minimums, and requirements before you invest. Always DO YOUR RESEARCH!

Abbott Labs (ABT)

Aetna Inc (AET)

Aqua America Inc (WTR)

AT&T Inc (T)

Automatic Data Processing, Inc. (ADP)

Banco Santander (SAN)

Bank of America (BAC)

Caterpillar (CAT)

CBS Corporation (CBS)

Chevron Corporation (CVX)

Coca-Cola Company (KO)

Colgate-Palmolive Inc (CL)

ConocoPhillips (COP)

Consolidated Edison Inc (ED)

Cummins Inc (CMI)

Exelon Corporation (EXC)

Exxon Mobil Corporation (XOM)

Ford Motor Co. (F)

General Electric (GE)

Hasbro (HAS)

Hewlett-Packard Company (HPQ)

Intel Corporation (INTC)

International Business Machines (IBM)

Johnson & Johnson (JNJ)

Kellogg Company (K)

Kohls Corporation (KSS)

McDonald's Corporation (MCD)

Mondelez International (MDLZ)

Paychex (PAYX)

The Procter & Gamble Company (PG)

Charles Schwab Corporation (SCHW)

Sherwin-Williams Company (SHW)

3M (MMM)

Verizon Communications Inc. (VZ)

Wal-Mart Stores Inc. (WMT)

Wells Fargo (WFC)

— And so many more, including a huge range of foreign companies….

6

······

Investment Examples with DRIPs

Using any one of the many compounding investment calculators available online, here are a few of examples of the potential returns of DRIPs over the long term assuming different investor timelines. (Please note: these numbers are only estimates based on growth averages and do not account for taxes or fees, but even with those conditions, I find them pretty compelling stats.)

EXAMPLE #1 (MID START INVESTING):

An investor (age 35) starts with $50 and contributes $50 per month in a DRIP account buying shares of an $82 stock that pays a 2.40% dividend yield. Assuming a modest 4% annual growth of the stock, and the reinvestment of all dividends, these are the possible returns, before taxes/fees.

- After ten years at age 45, the account would be worth $8,308.50.

- After 20 years at age 55, the account would be worth $24,253.12.

- After 30 years at age 65, the account would be worth $55,037.21.

This growth is possible with only $600 in annual contributions.

Adjusting those contributions to $100 per month (just $25 per week!) with the same details, the returns would look like this:

- After 10 years at age 45, the account would be worth $16,520.47.
- After 20 years at age 55, the account would be worth $48,319.85.
- After 30 years at age 65, the account would be worth $109,714.59.

Assuming $100 per month, but with a higher 6% annual growth, the returns would look like this:

- After ten years at age 45, the account would be worth $18,174.61.
- After 20 years at age 55, the account would be worth $60,301.34.
- After 30 years at age 65, the account would be worth $158,215.77.

With a higher $150 per month and 6% annual growth, the returns would look like this:

> After 30 years at age 65, the account would be worth $346,734.30.

- After ten years at age 45, the account would be worth $27,203.82.
- After 20 years at age 55, the account would be worth $90,316.96.
- After 30 years at age 65, the account would be worth $237,009.75.

At $50 per week, or $200 per month and 6.5% annual growth, the returns would look like this:

- After ten years at age 45, the account would be worth $37,110.92.
- After 20 years at age 55, the account would be worth $127,292.48.
- After 30 years at age 65, the account would be worth $346,734.30.

EXAMPLE #2 (EARLY START INVESTING):

An investor, age 25, starts with $50 and contributes $100 per month in a DRIP account buying shares of the same $82 stock that pays a 2.40% dividend yield. Assuming 7% annual growth of the stock, and the reinvestment of all dividends, these are the possible returns, before taxes/fees.

- After 15 years at age 40, the account would be worth $37,730.93.
- After 25 years at age 50, the account would be worth $115,041.92.
- After 35 years at age 60, the account would be worth $311,950.49.

At $200 per month ($50/week) and 7% annual growth, the returns would look like this:

- After 15 years at age 40, the account would be worth $75,258.63.
- After 25 years at age 50, the account would be worth $229,566.20.
- After 35 years at age 60, the account would be worth $622,582.57.

> With investors starting earlier, they have the power of compounding to help the growth of more modest investments.

EXAMPLE #3 (LATE START INVESTING):

An investor, age 55, starts with $50 and contributes $600 per month in a DRIP account buying shares of the same $82 stock that pays a 2.40% dividend yield. Assuming 6.5% annual growth of the stock, and the reinvestment of all dividends, these are the possible returns, before taxes/fees. [Note: A higher amount of investment should be possible because of peak earnings. With investors starting earlier, they have the power of compounding to help the growth of more modest investments.]

- After ten years at age 65, the account would be worth $111,089.41.
- After 15 years at age 70, the account would be worth $216,638.22.

At $800 per month ($200/week) and 7% annual growth, the returns would look like this:

- After ten years at age 65, the account would be worth $151,667.02.
- After 15 years at age 70, the account would be worth $300,424.80.

At $1000 per month ($250/week) and 7% annual growth, the returns would look like this:

- After ten years at age 65, the account would be worth $189,551.94.
- After 15 years at age 70, the account would be worth $375,480.19.

7

......

Final Thoughts

S o before we wrap up, let me share with you a few final thoughts. DRIPs can be part of an overall investment strategy that gets you closer to your retirement, freedom, or savings goals. For us, we'll keep adding to our DRIPs, and reinvesting the dividends until we need to cash out, or maybe just take all the dividends as income. One of our DRIP plans is essentially our daughters college fund, and another could be the nest egg lump we use to finish paying off the house once it gets to that point.

But consider these final suggestions:

- Always read the full prospectus of every DRIP plan, and never invest in anything you don't fully understand.
- If you want to invest in only one DRIP, that's fine, but consider you're diversification against all of your other investments.
- If you want to buy a few DRIPs, then mix and match sectors and industry. Try a bank, and a retailer, or a tech company, and a food producer. (WFC;

TGT; IBM; KRFT for example)

- Don't use DRIPs to speculate (I did once… and I regret it.)
- If a company stops paying a dividend, consider stopping your automatic investments. (Some even say to dump the holding, but I don't like to do that because it probably sold off after the announcement and I'd rather not sell on weakness.)

- If the market sells off hard, and you notice, it's possible to add extra shares, but it's usually better to just increase your monthly investment each time your budget allows it.

> # It's usually better to just increase your monthly investment each time your budget allows it.

- Always watch your fees. If the DRIPs aren't free, they can be as high as $2.50 transaction costs plus per share fees. If this is high compared to a small monthly investment, it might be better to look elsewhere. Of course, if you're investing a large enough amount, any fees can be nominal.

- Keep your records all in one place. Sales, taxes, and record-keeping around DRIPs are the myths to keep us all away from this style of investing. Don't believe the drama, but stay organized.

So best of luck with your money, your personal journey towards wealth, prosperity, and happiness, and your ongoing financial education…. and MINE!

8

......

DRIP and DSPP Resources

Dividend Reinvestment Plans and Direct Stock Purchase Plans (DRIP/ DSPP) Transfer Agents:

COMPUTERSHARE INVESTOR CENTRE

www.computershare.com

WELLS FARGO SHAREOWNER SERVICES

www.shareowneronline.com

AMERICAN STOCK TRANSFER & TRUST COMPANY

www.amstock.com

DEUTSCHE BANK GLOBAL DIRECT INVESTOR SERVICES

www.adr.db.com

JPM ADR

www.adr.com

And others

My Related Website:

DRIP INVESTING PLANS

www.dripinvestingplans.com

About the Author

Alan Kerrman is an individual investor who lives near Boston, Massachusetts, USA. He is NOT a finance professional and is NOT a registered investment advisor, but an enthusiastic and motivated retail trader, investor, writer, and full-time educator. He wants to succeed with his money, and wants to help you succeed with yours by sharing what he's learned about finance and investing along the way. He lives in an old New England house with his wife and daughter.

ALSO BY ALAN KERRMAN

• Trading Options on Tech Stocks: Selling Puts & Calls:

Real Examples to Generate Consistent Option Income and More and

• The Seven Step Rocket Start-Up Plan

Your Hard Truth Cheat Sheet for Starting Your Own Successful Small Business

.

Author's Note

I like to think of these author notes as my book 'extras' because you certainly do not have to read it, but if you do you'll get more insight into my process. This was a fun, rewarding, and fascinating book to write, but it feels like it could either be 10 pages or 500 pages long! I like to tell people about this stuff, so sharing it here in this book was a fulfilling process. Now obviously this is a short book — cut-to-the-chase short, I hope — but hopefully still well worth the investment of time and $$ on your part.

For me, the financial aspects of my personal family anecdotes stuff were hard to write (emotionally). And the numbers in the projection material were sometimes a little unruly, but I think in the end that there's some useful stuff here for everyone, even if you already hold DRIPs. That said, I had this book on pre-order for a little bit before it was published and I want to now personally THANK those 14 readers (yes, fourteen people... all in the United States and Canada), who believed in this project enough to pre-order it. THANK YOU, very much... Your orders — a cure for any possible writer's block — kept me very motivated!

I'd also like to add some notes here about the production, a few months later, of the paperback edition of this book. It's been an interesting and fulfilling process and was part of the plan all along. I had hoped to release the ebook and paperback versions at the same time, but life got in the way of that plan.

Specifically for this edition I have decided to include a topical index. I did that because most non-fiction books, especially finance, need another level of navigation other than the table of contents, and it just feels more complete. The other reason is that on tablets, smartphones, and laptops, readers can easily search through their ebooks directly, so this adds this for readers like you as well.

The cover is different, but related, to the original ebook edition. This was a combination of convenience, and also actual barriers in the design. The technical way the ebook cover was created would not make it possible to continue into a paperback binding (front, back, and spine), so it was necessary to start from scratch. I did, however, make sure to keep the same color profiles of the ebook so that the linked books are obvious online.

In terms of design, I also added several text 'call-outs' throughout the book. It's a design element -- almost magazine style -- that prepares the reader visually for some of the content on the page. It also serves to catch book 'browsers' who might flip through a book like this. For you, my wonderful reader, I hope that the call-out text makes it easier for you to share this copy of my book with others -- including loved ones, family members, and friends. I have been telling everyone I know all about DRIPs for years, so I know it's hard to get some people interested in the process of securing their financial future.

(I specifically share the 'potential' investing returns with every young (or younger) person I know and meet so that they consider automating their investing process now. For every parent or grandparent thinking about the future of a little one, a long-term DRIP account is a nice way to get a college fund, wedding money, or house payment together over a long period of time.

Lastly, I wanted to say that my books and ebooks, are also a part of my long-term investment strategy. How? I hope that these books not only help others -- including my family and friends -- but make enough residual sales and royalties over the years to eventually fund my daughter's DRIP plans directly. That would be the perfect scenario: long-term income-based dividend investing, with low fees, paid for by residual royalties from Daddy's time, energy and effort. Thanks for reading this, and best of luck with your financial world and the important stuff it affects.

— All best, A.K.

• Investing in DRIPs:
Using Dividend Reinvestment Plans to Achieve Financial Freedom

Please consider leaving a review of this book online, and thank you again for reading this!

INVESTING IN DRIPS

Index

3M (MMM), 45
401K plan, 10, 23, 31
403b plan, 17, 31

Abbott Labs (ABT), 43
ACH withdrawals, 9
Aetna (AET), 43
Alcatel-Lucent (ALU), 24
America Stock Transfer & Trust
        Company, 53
Apple (AAPL), 17, 28
Aqua America (WTR), 43
AT&T, Inc (T), 43
Automatic Data Processing (ADP),
        43

Banco Santander (SAN), 43
Bank of America, 43

Berkshire Hathaway (BRK.A), 17
Biogen Idec, 17
Bloomberg, 21
bonds, 17, 41
Boston, MA, 55

Canada, 57
capital losses, 25
casino, 26
Caterpillar (CAT), 44
CBS Corporation (CBS), 44
Chevron (CVX), 44
CNBC, 21
Coca Cola Company (KO), 44
Colgate-Palmolive (CL), 44
Computershare, 37, 53
ConocoPhillips (COP), 44
Consolidated Edison (ED), 44

61

racetrack, 26
registered investment adviser, 21, 55
Ramsey, Dave, 23
Roth IRA, 10
royalties, 58-59

Scottrade, 19
Schwab Corporation (SCHW), 44
"Seven Step Rocket Start-Up Plan,"
      56
shareholder meetings, 39
Sherwin-Williams (SHW), 45

Target (TGT), 52
TD Ameritrade, 19
Tesla, 28
"Trading Options on Tech Stocks,"
      55
transfer agents, 37, 53-54
transaction fees, 11
travel, 31

vacation, 39
Vanguard 500 Index Fund
      (VFINX), 19
Verizon Communications (VZ), 45

Wall Street insider, 21
Walmart (WMT), 41, 45
wedding,
Wells Fargo & Co., 17, 45, 51
Wells Fargo Shareowner Services,
      37, 53

Yahoo Finance, 38, 41

www.ingramcontent.com/pod-product-compliance
Lightning Source LLC
Chambersburg PA
CBHW021443170526
45164CB00001B/361